How To Find A Good Black Man

A Tome by

Theodore K. McClendon

Positive People Publishing
P.O. Box 4
Culver, IN 46511

Library of Congress Cataloging in Publication Data

McClendon, Theodore K., 1958-
How To Find A Good Black Man

I.   Relationships
II.   Women's Issues
III.   African-American Studies
IV.   Sociology/Psychology
V.   Self Help

ISBN# 0-9639329-1-8

How To Find A Good Black Man was written by
Theodore K. McClendon
Positive People Inc. GMI /TKM Copyright 1995

Cover Design: Julius Lyles III for JillyPig Productions
Cleveland, Ohio

Acknowledgements

To my parents for instilling the thirst for knowledge and for raising three decent and productive citizens. Mission accomplished.

Thanks to my brother Duane who is one of the smartest human beings on earth.

To Garrard who became an author and publisher when most people could only talk about it.

Thanks to my grandfather, the late Theodore Jones, who had ideas as big as those of the big CEO he chauffeured. Big Gramps! Peace.

Thank you Granny: the toughest little lady in North America who makes sweet potato pie so good it'll make you cry.

To Aunt Nel, for understanding my black sheep tendencies.

To Uncle Bill and Aunt Sylvia for the eclectic discussions and get-togethers.

To the late Uncle Nap, who had an incredible knowledge of real estate and who was always Big Fun.

My paternal grandparents for planting seeds of knowledge though I never met them.

To Lisa, may your blessings begin to flow more abundantly.

My cinema professors at L.A. City College, "yes, I'll use my film degree. I promise."

To Bobby Mardis for paying serious dues in the showbiz world. You 'bout ta git paid, Money!

To Sylvia, for teaching me the value of self-love. "God has got your back sista'."

To the Creator of the Universe for the Harmony of the Spheres.

Gratitude

...ston, Raymond W. Young, Michell Carter, SCDTVA, ...ool System, Maywood Little League, Purdue University--Hammond Campus, Dr. Kamalipour, Michael Robinson, Jeffrey Cusic and the Wabash Brothers--circa 1984-88, O.B. of the Four Tops, Laurie Selinger, Jeff Locke, Bill Judd, Kendall Hyatt, Marcia Daubner, Greg Nelson, Chris Mayer, the Baldufs, Lisa Nixon, Monica McKenna, Dave, Mary, Richetta, Cory, Bill, Ross, Chad, Karen, Todd, Laura K., Laura N., Tracey Traylor, C.J. and Bob, and the entire Ameritech Cellular Crew, Dr. J.P. Geuens, Dr. Robert Stahley, G.I. Bill, Ameen Y. Muhammad, Cassandra Griffin (our silent PARTNER), Carlotta King, Joanne Fultz, Rebe, The LACC Black Student Union circa 1983-1986, Lebo, Orland, Mike, Daoud, Nuri, Come-Ma-Ma and Mother Mildred, Arlene, Linda Brown, Diane Cook, Gina Murry, Michelle Lewis (Parlez-vous francais?), Bob Cooper, Deon Bradley, Saundra Kanardy, Johanna Sanders, Mark Green, Candace Baumgartner, The members of Seville: Herman Edwards, Mike Smith and Harlan Foster, Emil Vinet, The Morrow Family, Ernest Thomas, Muhammad Ali, Berry Gordy, and all who have touched my life.

Special Thanks

I offer the greatest thanks to my brother and publisher, Garrard McClendon. You know, it's a good thing to believe in yourself, but sometimes what we need more than anything is for one person, one soul, on this earth to believe in us also. No man is an island, someone once said. We cannot truly stand alone. We all need the love, encouragement, and support of others to ensure our victory in this life. We delude ourselves if we think we can make it totally on our own.

Garrard believed in me. He believed I had enough to say to write a book. He believed in, and supported, my idea of writing a genuine and soulful book. In so doing he made himself rare among publishers. No other publisher would have had the insight -- not to mention the courage -- to release a book like this one. The few who would have accepted my manuscript would surely have edited the soul out of the text. It would have been the watered-down version and we would have all suffered. But brave and confident Garrard said, "Let's put it out there and let the chips fall where they may." Consequently, we have a work that we both can be proud of.

I wish only the best for my brother the publisher. I hope that his talent to see the hidden treasure in unproven writers makes him the biggest and best publisher of all time. I hope that his company becomes a beacon for all writers(as well as readers) so that they may know that the human spirit, encapsulated in ink and paper, is one of the greatest forces on earth.

Bandleader, Gil Evans, said it best when he told the great jazz artist Miles Davis, "I sure am glad you were born." Garrard, I sure am glad you were born.

Peace, Teddy M.

To my son Maximilian:
May you dispel a thousand myths about the behavior and capabilities
of African-American males.

To my daughter, Miranda (Aurora):
May your heightened intuition navigate your journey.

To my niece, ReAnne (Namara), future supermodel
(circa 2007):
May your inner beauty continue to match your outer beauty.

To my nephew, Jaiman (Duane):
You've got some serious uncles on both your mother's and father's
sides. You've got to do big things, little man. It's in the plan,
understand?

This book was written for my daughter,
Olympia (Re'Jean),
who is coming of age.

Love Always,
Daddy

To a Lonely Sister

Empty pillow next to mine
rollin' over in the shadow of a fantasy;
a dream of a Black man coming to love and render
me speechless with one touch of his strong Black
hand...

I got my money,
I got my house...
But my house is not a home
and I still sleep alone.

Black man sleep next to me.

Raymond Thompson
(dnomyar)

...this is straight from the heart.

Felton Pilate III
Confunkshun

CONTENTS

FOOLED BY APPEARANCES

It is absolutely amazing how easy
it is to pick up women with such superficial things as
cars, jewelry, haircuts, clothes, and shoes. These
things -- and many others that I have not listed --
reveal merely the shell of a man. They are not the
man himself. Certainly,
a woman would hope that her prospect would have
nice things and look handsome as well. There is
nothing wrong with this, but it must
be strongly emphasized that even the most evil,
meanest, jivest cat in the world can show you
attractive material manifestations.

~

Indeed, in many cases it is just such a scoundrel who
will offer the most impressive display. He is skilled at
presenting you with decoys that get your attention
and lure you into his snares. He knows
that you like alligator

shoes (snake skin), socks with embroidered designs, and the dopest hoe pulling cologne. So he gives you a chance to take a good look at his wares. All the while, he is studying your interest level. The more you check him out, the more he's checking you out, checking him out. He patiently studies you until you begin giving him the non-verbal cues he needs to see. And when you do (give these signs) he engages his well-rehearsed program to get you where he wants you.

~

Basically lady, you're a sitting duck once you show that you are more concerned about the image than you are about the person behind the image. When a guy sees that kind of vibe coming from a woman he reciprocates the woman's superficiality with a brand of his own. Suddenly, you become a pair of breasts, a set of legs , and a beautiful derriere where there once might have been a thinking, caring, and sensitive individual. To the man, you are now an object, a plaything, a toy, a sport, and no amount of "intelligent conversation" can convince him otherwise. You've tipped your hand. You've shown him that you aren't "about" anything substantial and now his total focus is on the panties.

~

When a lady is driven by the things she sees, she is setting herself up for serious manipulation. Wasn't it Shakespeare who said "All the world's a stage?" Well, you can believe that, because indeed the world's a stage especially where male/female courtship and seduction are concerned. Men will write the most convincing scripts; fashion the most elaborate sets; utilize the most realistic props; employ the most outlandish wardrobe; hire the best supporting cast; just to create the scene (or scenes) that might persuade a woman into bed.

takes lady, he'll do it. But that's only w.... .
make yourself such an easy target. That's when you
show him you are governed by appearances. You
have the power to flip the script or, to better yet,
tear up the script. This isn't a movie. This is real life
so you should strive to keep the relationship "on-the-
real," especially at the crucial courtship/flirtation
stage.

~

How do you do this? You do this by showing interest
in the inner man. Get to the heart of the matter. Get
to know his heart and his mind. What's important to
him? Does he support a cause? What does he stand
for? Why, specifically, did his first marriage fail or
why did his last serious relationship fail? Does he
believe in monogamy? Does he enjoy the company
of children? Can he hold a lengthy, intelligent

conversation? Can he look a white man in the eye and relate intellectually? Does his television viewing expand beyond, say, sports, macho movies, or sitcoms? (Sure he watches HBO, ESPN, and BET, but does he also watch PBS?) What type of music does he like? Are his tastes balanced or heavily weighted in one musical direction? Can he cook, if necessary? Is he neat, semi-neat, semi-messy, or totally disorganized? Can the brother spell? If not, does he have adequate comfort and facility with the dictionary? Has he had a broken heart? More importantly, has he broken any? Where did he grow up? How did he grow up? Who is his best friend? On what level does he relate to his friend? Does he live near any of his ex-ladies? Does he see any of his ex-ladies? Is he down with the struggle? In what capacity is he fighting in the struggle? Can he relate to and get along with whites without coming across as a total handkerchief head-scratching buffoon-a-Tom ? Does he even sense a need for such racial balance? Does his mother like you? Does she respect you? Has he ever dated a white woman? Would he? Does he glance at blondes in your presence? Who's his childhood hero? Who's his current hero? What would his ideal wife be like? What is his religion? If organized religion is not his preference, does he believe in God?

~

Do you ask all of these questions on the first date? Of course not. We know how foolishly overbearing that would be. But do you begin to ask a few of these types of questions on the first date? Definitely! In fact, don't wait for the first date. Let the questions begin at the first encounter. Try breaking the ice with this one some time: "Do you believe in God?" Yeah, get the ball rolling with that one. Oh, so you think that's a joke? Okay, fine, but don't run crying to your friends and family when your fine boyfriend confesses his atheism to you, in thought or in action. Suddenly, that question doesn't seem so stupid! Does it? The point is, there are some incredibly important facts you need to know about a potential companion. And though you can get many questions answered through observation and women's intuition, some questions must be answered verbally by the man himself. And you, dear one, must ask those questions.

~

Don't fall in love with an image.
Many brothers portray an image: a facade.
Images are often mirages: they disintegrate upon close inspection. Inspect that brother closely.
Acknowledge that you were enticed by his image; it's what attracted you to the guy in the first place.

But as you are pulled closer into his space, get yourself a good, clean, and unclouded look into his life. Look into his very being -- his core. Make this your close encounter of the third kind. Make contact with his essence. Dance with his soul. Draw nearer to the man within the man. Soar with his spirit. Feel the rhythm of his distant drummer and listen for the still, small voice. Seek out the him that was a him before there was a him.

~

Welcome to the Far Out Psychic Federation! Just kidding ladies, but understand this: ultimately you will come to know the soul of this man. It's best to begin your search at the front end of the relationship.

~

How do you make this spiritual connection? I can give you a clue and point you in the right direction.

Ask questions and wait for replies while looking deep into his eyes. Look into his eyes. Study his eyes. The eyes don't lie. The eyes, it is said, are the windows of the soul. Look through the windows; through them and not at them. Look through the windows of his soul.

~

Does this seem a little deep for you? I'm sorry, but love is deep. Relationships are deep. Life is deep. Maybe it's time you left the shallows anyway. Happiness is deep, to be sure.

~

YOU PROBABLY WALKED RIGHT BY HIM

A big, big problem that a lot of Black females have is speaking to Black men as they walk by in public. Some of you find it entirely too painful to utter a simple "hello" to the half-a-dozen or so decent African-American men you see everyday. Granted, you've been approached by more than your share of limp-pimping, crotch-holding knuckleheads and it is easy to understand a certain wariness you may feel toward encounters with Black men in general, but you simply cannot close yourself off from the entire lot of decent, eligible brothers. You've got to get into the habit of speaking to all Black men who acknowledge you and carry themselves in a dignified manner.

~

I'm reminded of my college days when I'd be traversing the campus from one hall to the next and I'd come across a Black female approaching me from the opposite direction. More often than not, I would get ignored entirely. Other times, I'd get a condescending sneer. Sometimes I'd get a reluctantly mumbled "hello." Every so often I'd get a respectfully knowing nod. And once in a blue moon, I'd hear one of these sisters emote a cheerful "how ya' doin'."

~

I used to wonder, "what's the deal with these ladies?" Granted, I wasn't dressed in a business suit at the time and obviously I didn't have a yuppie mobile in the lot, but I wore clean clothes and my body hygiene was always in check. Moreover, I was in an institution of higher learning trying to better myself and advance my standing in society. Yet I couldn't rate a simple "hello" from someone who should've been glad I was there. What kind of warped sense of direction does a sister have to possess to dis an up and coming brother like that?

~

Ah, but fast forward this picture a few short years into the future. I revisit my alma mater to pick up some tickets to a seminar. I'm dressed in that business suit, the brief case is in tow. The yuppie mobile indeed is in the lot. Suddenly I get more greetings than a visiting dignitary. Come on! I'm the same guy! The very same guy! In fact, I might have been an even better guy while matriculating as an under grad, because corporate America hadn't yet dampened my youthful, student idealism. Now I get all the play 'cause I look like I might be somebody. I was somebody in my jeans, my book bag, and my clean Earth, Wind, & Fire T-shirt, but very few (very,very few) young women took the time to even try to find out.

~

Are you guilty of this kind of knee jerk behavior? Are you cold dissing brothers left and right because they don't look like Black Enterprise incarnate? If you are, then I submit to you that you may be cutting out an entire segment of eligible and qualified young men that could well contain your true life's companion. Now if you want a cardboard cut out, picture-perfect, pretty boy brother to fill the void in your life, then so be it. Knock yourself out, but don't expect him to be your Mr. Right. Take this guy to parties, show him off to your friends, but forget about getting serious with this guy. He's a mannequin, not a man. Is that what you really want?

~

I hate to burst your bubble lady, but your ultimate man may well be a guy that you would have heretofore called a nerd. When I say this, I don't necessarily refer to his having buck teeth, high water pants, and pop bottle glasses with tape on the bridge. Hopefully he won't be that far gone, but it's probably safe to say that he won't be exactly camera-ready material for GQ either. At first glance, he'll probably be very "regular." He'll more than likely be a "Plain Wayne -- Joe Average" to the naked eye. But you cannot be overly influenced by this. Go beyond the image and delve into the man. What's in his conversation? Where is he coming from?

~

Suddenly, you realize that what you once would have thought was a total nerd can turn out to be quite an interesting character. And that's really what you want: a man who has character, not a mechanized wax figure. More specifically, you want and need a man with character.

16

~

You need a man who is "about something," and most men who are about something have graduated above the immature stage of trying to be hip. They have probably also gotten over the hang up of trying to be pretty. Because now they know that real hipness is being legitimately knowledgeable about things and real attractiveness entails being truly in touch with one's self. A man in touch with his true self is a beautiful being. This type of man goes light years beyond being merely fine. He's the whole package: the real man.

~

It has come to be cliche' in this day in age, but it really is true that inner beauty is more important than outer beauty. Yeah, yeah, I know you're saying "but I don't want no Godzilla either." Granted, I can respect that. Chances are, your prospect won't look like a hideous monster anyway, but it's equally likely that he won't look like Denzel or Snipes either. So don't avoid the brother if he doesn't look like a movie star. Besides, you probably aren't exactly Halle Berry or Cindy Crawford your damned self!

~

Rise above your conditioned tendency to dis the African-American male. Reintroduce yourself to the reality of his humanity. He has feelings, hopes, dreams, and fears just like you do. Get out of the habit of thinking you are too good for him. This is the blatant, self-deluding lie you've been telling yourself for far too long. You are not better than him, and you shouldn't even want to be better than him. You should want to be his partner, his companion, his equal -- if you will.

~

However, if this is not what you want to be then it is no surprise to know that you're still alone and no mystery to learn that you probably walked right by him.

~

SECRETLY,
YOU WANT A DOG

As strange as it may sound, some good women out there really don't want a good man. They want a brother who is going to be somewhat shady and somewhat slick. They want a slightly underhanded guy who will keep them on their toes, keep them guessing, and ultimately keep them "manless."

~

I am at a loss to explain the psychology behind this peculiar phenomenon so I really should defer to you -- my female reader -- for a little consultation on this matter. It's a total mystery to most men why some women who claim to be earnestly seeking a trustworthy male companion seem to gravitate toward dudes who are unadulterated dogs.

~

To venture an educated guess, I'd say it has something to do with excitement. Suave and dashing guys with hidden agendas and roaming eyes are exciting to a lot of women. They offer a thrill component that's not always readily forthcoming in the dutiful husband type. Not being a psychologist, I'd venture further by saying this phenomenon would be somewhat closely akin to the peculiar love some people have for roller coasters, scary movies, and bungy jumping. They will go out of their way to be mortally terrified to within an inch of their lives just to have a "good time." I think you see the connection.

~

On some level I can accept this thrill-seeking mentality and I feel its harmless enough in the context of casual dating, but when it comes down to seriously seeking a mate -- this thrill-seeking bologna has got to go! Listen ladies, you need a companion -- not a 3-ring circus. Get it right! Besides, why would you even want a relationship that could be considered analogous to a roller coaster ride? Do you really want your love to be filled with peaks, valleys, and unpredictable twists? Of course not. What you want -- rather what you need -- is a love that's like a cruise. You need to be sailing on into a glorious horizon.

~

If cruising sounds too boring for you, fine, go ahead and take in some more thrills, but inevitably you'll be back to square one saying: "I need a man.
I need me a huzzbon."

~

Another curious female mind set
which is even more bizarre than the thrill-seeking syndrome is the "he's too nice" mentality. Now, how can a guy be too nice? I first learned of this mentality when I was about a sophomore in high

school (over twenty years ago). A girl who I was absolutely infatuated with and had been dating for several months came to me one day and said, soberly, " I don't think I wanna go with you no more." Shocked and disheartened I asked her "why not?" She replied tersely, "Because you're too nice." This totally blew my mind and I'm still reeling from the initial jolt of that statement to this day.

~

Too nice? How can someone be too nice? Shouldn't you want someone in your life who is kind, considerate, and trustworthy? I would think that that would be the goal. Indeed, it should be the goal to have a sincere and good-hearted significant other in your life. To have a partner who genuinely has your best interest at heart should be one of your highest aspirations and most fervent desires. To be with a person who will help you face the difficulties of life should be the crowning glory of your existence, yet so many women run away from such a beautiful blessing.

~

Certainly it is understandable that you would not want to share your life with an overly docile and wimpy "yes man." Naturally you want a man with backbone. That's a given, but you must be insightful enough to know the difference between a nice person and a sap. The two aren't necessarily synonymous. A guy can be extremely nice and kind without being a totally gullible sucker of a man. Certainly, you've heard the term "gentleman"? Well, that is what I am speaking of: a personable good-hearted person.   A gentleman is considerate, but he isn't a pushover or a sap. He will do his best to be diplomatic and fair minded but if you try to cross him, you will quickly be reminded of his level of self-respect and his constitutional integrity. In plainer words, he won't let anyone walk on him.

~

On the other hand, there are so-called men out there who will let you disrespect them. This type of man has no problem trading his backbone for the adoration of his mate. The term "henpecked" comes immediately to mind. Of course you should avoid this type of spineless character, but again you've got to know the difference between this amoeba-like creature and an authentic gentleman. Some differences are blatant, but others are often quite subtle.

~

If you do not train yourself to become more sensitive to the intricate nuances of male behavior, then you will forever misinterpret the various signs and clues that could help you get the picture regarding what to look for in a mate. You can't continue to employ your same old set criteria for "reading" Black men. Chances are you're probably way off the mark.

~

I could probably give examples from here to Pluto citing the differences between a gentleman and a sucker, but the following little humorous role-play gently sums up the essence of the matter.

You: "Hey, baby. Can you massage my back, rub my feet, wash the dishes, cut the grass, buy me something, run my bath water, cook my dinner, cuddle up with me, help me with my bills and...[generally] worship the ground I walk on?"

Sucker: "Yes dear."

Gentleman: "Yes dear, and tomorrow can you massage my back, rub my feet, wash the dishes, vacuum my ride, buy me that CD, scratch my dandruff, cook my dinner, run my bath water and wear that thong I bought you from Frederick's?"

27

~

To be sure, a gentleman is nice to you, but he is also nice to himself.

~

Ah, but let's bring this full circle and revisit the reason I wrote this chapter in the first place. Secretly you have wanted and craved for a dog because you couldn't tell the difference between a gentleman and a sap. You thought they were one in the same, so you went out to find a man who could put you "in your place," so to speak. It goes without saying that a dog will definitely let you know where he's coming from and though you don't necessarily go for his methods, you do respect his guts. We sum it up by saying, you really do not want a doggish scoundrel for a man, and obviously you don't want a punk. You want a gentleman. So go ahead and say it: "I *want a gentleman."*

~

Right on, sista!

WHY SOME BROTHERS *OPT* FOR WHITE BABES

Yeah, let's just vibe on that chapter title for a minute. Put the book down and just reflect on the overall concept of "Jungle Fever" and we'll pick it back up in a few. Is that cool with you?

Boy oh boy! What a can of worms this is, but let's dive right in. Shall we? If I've seen it once, I've seen it a thousand times. A brother is out on a date with a white woman and the sisters in the area are burning a hole in the couple with laser-like stares. The sisters glare at the guy and sneer at the white woman as if to say, "brother, you sold yourself out," and "bitch, there ain't no shortage of White men out here. Why y'all gotta' take all our men?" You know the story. You might even be one of these sideline hecklers yourself. I don't know.

Brothers do the same thing when they are similarly "confronted" with the presence of a Black woman/white man couple. It's a trip and it's something that we have to stop trippin' on. But these feelings are real and we'll have to work through them at some point.

~

Okay, so you're standing there fuming and trying to show that "Uncle Tom" just how pissed off you are. Currently, you're not only waiting to exhale; you're about to explode! However, you should really take time out to analyze the situation. You need to seriously grapple with the reasons why brothers take the blonde plunge.

~

First of all, there's a school of thought which suggests that the modern day Black man pursues White women now just because he _can_. That is, he subconsciously knows that in past eras miscegenation (interracial mating) was strictly taboo. Indeed it was something punishable with death, flogging, humiliation, or worse,...castration. Nevertheless, times have changed and he knows this. He realizes that even though there is theoretical opposition to interracial relationships, the harsh physical consequences are a thing of the past. So in some cases as an act of utter belligerence, a Black man will date, seduce, or marry a white woman. Some Black men absolutely relish the thought of "taking" the white woman from the white man. It's a payback (of sorts) for the long centuries of oppression that Blacks have had to face here in this country. It's a highly visible way of saying "F____ you, slave master!"

~

Personally, I don't subscribe to this mind set but it's

definitely a mode of thinking in some African-American male circles.

~

Another school of thought regarding the question of why Black men show interest in white women is in the area of moral support. That is, some Black men feel that white women are much more sensitive to the hopes, fears, and dreams of the Black man. Some brothers go so far as to say that white women are even more "down-with-the-struggle" than most Black women.

~

Now don't you all jump on me at once, but I can kind of see where that sentiment is coming from! You know, sisters can get pretty harsh on a man's feelings. Sometimes, some Black women can be a little bit too boisterous and testy for their own good (not to mention the good of the relationship). Some

Black women think nothing of shattering a brother's dream with sarcastic comments and incredulous looks. I've often found myself in relationships where I'd be doing something constructive to enhance my intelligence or awareness and I'd get ridiculed and discouraged with comments like "what you doing that for?" or "you need to quit." I can distinctively remember an incident I had in one relationship that speaks to this issue.

~

I loved this woman very, very much and I had planned on being with her for the rest of my life, but it was becoming apparent that she wasn't quite on the same page with me philosophically or intellectually. One evening as I sat in my chair to unwind, I tuned into one of my "educational" channels on cable television. I cannot recall whether it was "The Learning Channel," "Arts &

Entertainment," or simply PBS, but a highly interesting documentary (to me at least) was on and I was thoroughly engrossed in the program. [I think the subject matter was the cutting edge research being done in the area of superconductivity and the unbelievable breakthroughs in transportation, communication, and health care that this research will one day yield]. With my undivided attention on the screen, this woman approaches me and says: "Why do you always watch those boring Discovery channel shows?" I replied, "Oh my fault. Let me tune into Wheel of Fortune. That's certainly more exciting!" I'm kidding, but what I did say was. "I happen to think that this is an interesting show and you shouldn't be doggin' me out when I'm trying to develop my mind."

She chuckled caustically and walked out of the room. This hurt me to the core not only because the woman of my dreams dissed my intellectual progress, but also because we as a people have seemed to have lost our thirst for knowledge in general. This woman should have been delighted that her man was on a path to higher knowledge but she chose to cut me down for my diligence.

~

So what does this have to do with the subject of white women? Well, my sister, I hate to say this, but I don't think I would have gotten this kind of flack from a white babe. Straight up.
Oh boy, now I've done it. Allow me to clarify. On average, I'd venture to say that the average white lady would be more understanding in situations like the aforementioned than a sister.

~

Don't misconstrue this observation and don't take it personally. There are forces at work which contribute to white women being more sensitive to the emotional needs of Black men. The shoe fits the other foot as well. White men in many cases may seem "nicer" than Black men. The forces that make this so are economics, history, family background, social environment and media depiction. These all relate to the roots of self-esteem. It is much easier to be nice as well as understanding when you come from an intelligent, well-balanced and nurturing background. As a whole, the skills, gifts, talents, hopes, and aspirations of whites are valued and nurtured at an exponentially higher level than those of African-American people. This is especially true of our disparate early life experiences. Again, I speak about the typical. It should go without saying that there are exceptions.

~

The end result is that a Black man feels he can get

more emotional and intellectual support from his white woman.

~

Now there are two ways you can take this reality. On the one hand, you can do what many of your peers would do; get angry. Or, on the other hand, you can use the phenomenon of interracial dating as a learning tool. You could go out and make a concerted effort to find out the various reasons why Black men pursue white women. You could consult library publications or better yet, you could ask someone you know in an interracial relationship why they have chosen to go that route. Information gleaned from such an inquiry might enlighten you to things you may have never contemplated. Granted, you might not know all the answers and the answers you do get from your research might be somewhat disturbing, but you'll come out as a better person.

You will have the benefit of knowledge on your side. You won't have to go the ignorant route of being ticked off by people with "Jungle Fever" anymore. You will have the silent, inner awareness that these two people just might be together for reasons that transcend race. What an interesting thought.

~

UNDERSTANDING THE PLIGHT OF THE BLACK MAN

African-American people -- despite the incredible strides made in the area of basic civil rights -- are basically catching an awful lot of hell today in America. To most Blacks this is no secret at all. We know the playing field is uneven and the (proverbial) deck is stacked dauntingly against us. Affirmative action notwithstanding, it is still much easier to be white (or close to it) than it is to be Black in the modern-day United States of America. This is common knowledge to most of my African-American brothers and sisters.

~

[It must be noted here that opportunities for Blacks are greater now than they have ever been in the entire history of this nation, and I am in no way advocating a spirit of victimization or apathy among African-American people. Quite the contrary. At heart I am a believer in the "bootstrap" self-help concept of living and striving in this country. I believe Blacks must exert more effort toward

becoming more self-reliant, fiscally responsible and globally aware. Our people must try much harder in all areas of positive human endeavor. Crying "racism" at every disappointment or setback is not something that I support in the least.]
NONETHELESS...

~

Racism is alive and extremely well in America. We feel it's aggravating sting on a daily (if not hourly) basis. It is the unseen and unspoken law of the land. Black women say they are hardest hit by racism because very often they are the ones left to raise children and make a living alone in the white-dominated work-a-day world. They also say that it's a double whammy being both Black and female. They argue that the gender issue can often be as challenging as the question of race. And on some level
they are right.

~

43

On the other hand, Black men say they are
the ones hardest hit by racism. They cite the media
as being the primary perpetrator in the undermining
of the integrity of the African-American male.

Because of the reinforcement of negative
stereotypes in the media, Black males are viewed as
the most detrimental element in American society. As
a result, they are the most hated and feared group in
the nation (if not the world). On the "most hated
and feared scale," the African-American male is
somewhere between the Norway rat and the great
white shark. The perception is almost that bad. So it
follows then that the Black man feels he has it worse
than the Black woman. On some level _he_ is right.

~

Actually, Black women and men are equally
right, but what has been lacking is a deeper concern
and understanding for each other's plight. I can

merely empathize with the plight of Black women, but I can tell you first hand the type of snares and inconveniences which litter my walk as a Black man on a daily basis in America. I can only give you a glimpse or sampling of the almost infinite slings and arrows that are delivered to the consciousness of the African-American male, but hopefully these examples will elucidate the point.

~

To be Black is to be insulted. This is the conclusion at which my adult life in America has forced me to arrive. Not a day passes when someone (of any race) doesn't question either my intelligence, my integrity, my disposition, my job worthiness, my temperament, my sanity, or even my very right to exist. Invariably some situation will arise during the course of a day which will place at least one of the aforementioned attributes in question. Whether most

Black men want to admit this or not, they spend much of their public waking hours on the defensive. We walk in the silent knowledge that the public at large views us as buffoons, coons, incompetents, and latent criminals. This is ever intensified and complicated by the sad reality that some Black men (a very small, but very animated minority) actually are buffoons. Mind you, there are ignoramuses, buffoons, and knuckleheads in every race, but somehow other races don't have to bear the weighty burden of their undesirable members the way the African-American is forced to by society at large. For some strange reason, decent Black men are judged by the stupid actions of a few ignorant Negroes scattered throughout American society. White men are not judged in this way. Whites are able to detach themselves from the unsavory elements within their race. The pathologies of their criminal class do not impact upon their overall image as a people. When you tune into the five o'clock news and see the white serial rapist or ax murderer, we are not generally inclined to blame the whole white race for the conduct of a few white lunatics. Yet, let there be a drug bust or a gang killing on the very same news broadcast and the inference is clear: all Blacks are criminals. I know it's a sad reality but this is the type of image bashing propaganda that we're up against.

~

Some of you are thinking, "come on, it's not as bad as Black men say it is." Well let me tell you a little story and you can draw your own conclusion.

Recently a young white mother admitted to killing her two toddler-aged sons. For several days (prior to her confession of the murders) the young woman strung police and the American public along, with a concocted story of her being car-jacked by a Black man. Why did it have to be a Black man? Obviously, she wanted to come up with a story that was as convincing as possible. She knew (despite her lack of maturity and intelligence) that the American public -- fever pitched with politician-induced "anti-crime" sentiment -- would more readily buy her far-fetched story if she said the suspect was a Black man.

~

This is really a sad commentary on the general consensus of the American population. It says if you want to weasel your way out of a criminal mess just blame a Black man. This is disgusting! What is more, suppose the young mother had held her story together long enough for the authorities to go on a serious man hunt. And what if this man hunt would have turned up a man who met this woman's fabricated description?

~

You guessed it, some innocent brother, would
be on his way to death row. That innocent Black
man could've been your cousin, your boyfriend, your
son, or your dad. He'd still be on his way to the
gallows. Do you get the drift?

~

The deck is stacked so tough against the
Black man that it's a wonder that anyone of us is
still sane. Yet there are millions of brothers out there
who are doing their best to be decent, productive
citizens despite the overwhelming societal
impediments. These men must be applauded. They
must be held in high esteem, for they are a definitive
testament to the power and resiliency of the human
spirit.

~

YOUR KIDS

No man wants to be saddled with the unenviable burden of being the step-father of an unruly derelict of a child. If you have two or three derelicts, forget it altogether! The absolute worse thing men dread to see in a prospective mate (worse than her having lizard feet) is her having children who are undisciplined. A lot of women don't quite understand this too well. They believe that just because a man can't deal with their kids, he doesn't like kids at all. Women like this tell their friends, "Most men don't like women with children." This is an unfair and untrue statement. Quite the contrary, most men like kids a lot, but they do not like incorrigible brats! There is a difference, you know.

~

Men like children who mind their mother. Men like children who speak understandable English. Men like children who help with the chores. Men like children who respect adults. Men enjoy children who have hobbies and interests. Men appreciate children who empathize with the struggles of their mother. Men embrace children who try to understand the travails of their father. Men like children who share and who are optimistic. Courteous and kind children who know how to act in public are revered by men.

~

If your male friends have a tendency to "frown up" around your kids it's not necessarily because they dislike children. You just may have the type of children that only a mother could love. Step back and take a silent, detached look at your offspring. Are they the type of people you would enjoy spending time with if you were not related to them? Tell the truth? What are your kids really like? Do yourself a favor and make an objective assessment of your children's behavior and make adjustments if necessary. Be honest with yourself, or if it's just too close for you to truly see, ask an outside party to give you a report about the conduct of your kids. Tell them that you want to hear the truth (the whole truth) about the way your children are perceived by outsiders. You may hear some things that will hurt a little bit, but don't get defensive. This could be some of the best guidance you'll ever get if you'd just stick it out. Hang in there while you listen to the criticism. This is "tough love," to be sure, but it will serve you and your children for a lifetime.

~

Having clean, obedient and pleasant children should be its own reward, but the additional bonus you get is that men will respect and admire you more if your kids are trained. The key word here is respect, because some men will still stay around you -- bad kids and all -- just so they can take you to bed. Many fellows hang with women with brats if the sex is good enough, but you should have more respect for yourself, your children, and your man than that.

~

Work with your kids. A little attention goes a long way. Groom, grill, test, challenge, reward, admonish, and teach them. You are their model and mentor, not just their provider. You are the guardian of their souls until they reach the age of maturity. Your job is to impart as much knowledge, wisdom, and spirituality as is humanly possible to your children, so that they may be adequately armed to prevail in a world filled with hatred, ignorance, and deceit.

~

A woman who has well groomed and well trained children is beautiful. Through the good behavior of her children, she shows the world that she cares a great deal about humanity. To raise decent citizens in this society is no mean feat, and discerning men can easily see when a woman is making a sincere effort at pro-active child rearing. A man is usually more willing to step in and help the mother who demonstrates a definite desire to rear her children right, than if she were only going through the motions of parenting.

~

HIS MONEY

If you have a preconceived notion as to how much money your prospective lover has to make in order to get with you, you might as well head to the store and buy yourself a T-shirt that says in bold letters on the front, PROSTITUTE. If you really believe that money makes the man, sister, you are making the biggest mistake imaginable in your search for love. What you are saying in essence -- when you have a specific money qualification for a man -- is that you are for sale. So better yet, get a T-shirt that states, I'M FOR SALE.

~

That's not to say that you should disregard money or to seek out a poor man. This isn't being said at all here. Money is necessary to our mortal existence. It is the force that fuels most of our creature needs and is the engine that propels our society. Without it, we are but wandering vagabonds. The overwhelming concerns of our lives in the majority of human affairs revolve around the almighty dollar.

~

Understood, but despite the mortal omnipotence of money, there is one thing that exists in humanity that is even more all-powerful. And that, dear reader, is the human soul.

~

Quoting First John 4:4:
Greater is he that is in you, than he that is in the world.

This is a true testament to the power of the human and holy spirit. This power exists in us all but far too few people truly understand and believe this. It is much easier to trust in things "which do appear," but blessed are those who don't see yet still believe. That is why many of you will opt for the brother in the Seville STS or Lexus over the man with a Metro or bus pass. Using your eyes and logic, the obvious choice would be the man in the fine luxury automobile and nice home. Granted, but where in that equation is the "soul factor"? Have you sought it? Do you even care at this point? You should.

~

Listen, once again. I'm not knocking money and nice things, but consider this: to a rich man without scruples you just may be merely another one of his "nice" things. He might not even view you as a person at all. To him, you might be a mere possession. But could you really blame him if this rich man felt this way about you? After all, you would probably view him as a possession as well (A big bag of money).

~

Are you for sale, sister? Can your love and sex be bought by a man? Are you holding out for the highest bidder for the rights to your affection? Can you be auctioned? If so lady, consider this a forewarning:

YOU ARE DESTINED TO BE A DISILLUSIONED AND UNHAPPY WOMAN.

~

I hate to be the bearer of bad news, but money truly cannot buy you happiness. It's as true today as it ever was. It is especially true if the money isn't even yours. If the money is his, it will more than likely buy you sadness, heartache, and servitude.

~

The picture is quite different when you and your man build wealth together. In this scenario, the chances are good that your relationship has a more solid foundation. Obviously you married the man for more substantial reasons than just money. He wasn't rich when you met him but you saw his positive attributes. You saw his character and maybe (just maybe) you even took a glimpse at his soul. With what this man could do for you monetarily, you were not preoccupied. You wanted him for him. So the fact that later in the relationship the two of you did the necessary planning and legwork to create a degree of prosperity is strictly a bonus. In such a case, it is plain to see that money would then be a blessing, and indeed a basis for further happiness. However, it must be pointed out that money is just the bonus, or icing on the cake. The cake itself is love, faith, and cooperation between the man and the woman.

~

It is said that everyone has their price. You are probably no exception. If this is the case, here is some realistic advice based on common sense. [First let me state that ideally you should never sell out in any

circumstance, but hey, you're only human. Right?]
For the right price you can sell your beauty; you can
sell your booty; and you can sell your womanly
charms. But never, ever sell your dignity. Never sell
your soul! You might be thinking, "but am I not
selling my soul if I sell my body?" Not necessarily.
To some extent, housewives are doing just that, albeit
in a sanctioned and sanitized manner. When a
woman becomes a housewife she indeed is selling
her beauty, body, lovingkindness, and charms, not to
mention her organizational, managerial, and
culinary skills. But if she is living right, that is if she is
abiding by the guidelines set forth in Proverbs 31, she
is not selling out her soul at all. If she is living right,
she will get the utmost respect from both her
husband (if he is a decent man) and the greater
community at large. This is far from selling out.
On the other hand, if a woman is giving up her goods

just for the money, she is indeed selling her soul. She is no more than a merchant -- relying on barter and exchange. More precisely, she is at once, merchant and <u>merchandise</u>.

~

Concluding this chapter, let's look at the most effective strategy to avoid being a sellout or prostitute. GO DUTCH TREAT whenever and wherever possible. Buy your own stuff and let him buy his. Let the real reward be your togetherness. Stay out of his pocket (and make doubly sure he stays out of yours). Enjoy each other's company, not each other's checkbooks. If his male ego won't allow the woman to co-finance an evening date then give him your share of the expenses "off the scene." That is, you can go ahead and let him look like he is footing the bill while in reality you are sharing the costs. Defacto Dutch treat, if you will.

~

Your parents were right when they said, "if he buys you expensive meals and nice gifts, he expects something in return." It's human nature, no matter how much we men try to deny it. Simply put, "...if I wine and dine you, I wanna bump and grind you." Bottom line. However, you can totally subvert those types of intentions by going Dutch treat. It miraculously keeps things honest . Not only that, it also allows you to have even more expensive meals and lavish dates, based on your "collective" buying power. Besides, most contemporary couples eventually combine incomes anyway. Start this on the front end of the relationship.

~

Dutch treating just makes good sense all the way around. It keeps your dignity in tact, it keeps his ego in check, and it keeps the focus on the things that really matter, namely, one another's true selves.

~

Unless you only want to be another one of his "playthings," be very wary of spending his money.

~

WOMEN: CHAMPIONS OF DIRTY TALK

Much is ballyhooed about the fabled conversations that occur among men during a boys night out. All it takes is for an attractive, well-endowed female to walk by (or appear on the television screen, if the fellas' have chosen to watch a game or something) to trigger the simmering, collective pool of testosterone to come to a full, unrestricted boil. Once this hormonal volcano erupts within an ensemble of healthy, red-blooded, heterosexual, American males, it's usually not long before the locker room chatter begins.

~

Locker room talk (i.e: crude and explicit conversation about anticipated, or hoped for sexual contact with women, real or imagined) is generally engaged in by men in a spirit of fun. Most of what is said is indeed insulting, vulgar, and demeaning to women, but it is delivered in such a crude, and clumsy fashion that it becomes virtually innocuous to all but the most emotionally delicate females who might happen to find themselves within earshot of this basically benign boys-only banter.

~

Women have men fooled into believing that locker room talk is some kind of heinous crime. You've got men pretending to be choir boys in the presence of women. Men are afraid of being thought of as barbarians if they were to dare utter something that would be considered inappropriate for a "mixed company" assemblage. We gingerly walk on eggshells of false modesty and forced decorum in these situations while unbeknownst to us, there is nothing we could even dream up in a sexual vain that could do so much as approach the graphic, no-holds barred, sex chatter that comprises women's girl talk.

~

Compared to girl talk, locker room conversation is rated G. Well maybe PG or R (to the triple XXX rating of girl talk). It is some of the most seething, searing, caustic, explicit, defaming, embarrassing, lewd, insidious, lascivious, demeaning, defiling, repulsive conversation a man could ever hear. It's too deep! As a matter of fact, for the benefit of my male readers, I'm going to try to elucidate just how deep girl talk truly is. Fellas', there is a little exercise that I've devised to try to make the point about the bizarre sexual conversations and thought processes of women. Let us proceed! Shall we?

~

Gentlemen, picture the most outlandish scene you can imagine with your wife or significant other (or any female you might happen to fancy). Go into the most detail visionable. Make this thought as far

flung and freaky as you can.
[You may put the book down and further reflect on this request at this time].

~

Okay -- you got it? Good. Now hold that thought; multiply it by one thousand; amplify it by an order of magnitude and raise it to the tenth power and you might -- just might -- have an idea how expansive the sexual imagination of a woman is. Oh, so you say your loving wife or precious fiancee' doesn't think like that?! Brother, brother, brother, take my word for it, she does. As a matter of fact, raise that to the "n"th degree! They can't deny it without lying. A Spike Lee film offers the viewer a taste of girl talk with one lady stating that she would like to have a man with "a Zulu d____ down to his knees." The women who you least suspect of having those kinds of thoughts are the very ones with the most vivid imaginations. I don't know why my brother, but that's just the way it is. Deal with it.

We all have to.

~

If you still will not accept the possibility (reality) of your lady's imagination being exponentially more expanded than your own, here is some advice. Familiarize yourself with a handful of therapists from your handy yellow pages. Write their names and numbers down and keep them in your wallet. Hopefully, you'll never need this list, but if you happen to be unlucky enough to hear the things your lady says (about you and other men) in girl talk, you'll be absolutely feenin' for therapy.

~

Yes, it hurts. It hurts bad. It changes your life, forever.

~

Am I right ladies? You know just how serious it is?

~

So, all that being said, what can we learn from this phenomenon? Why is this chapter on dirty talk even important in the context of a book that deals with trying to find a man? Well, this subject is crucial, especially where it relates to keeping a man once you have found him. What you must try to do is bring your man into your realm of thinking. You need to bring him in as a participant, not merely as a subject, in your girl talk conversation. Intimate details that you share with your girl friends need to be shared with your man. Secret desires, fantasies, and complaints can do you little good in the ears of your nosy and miserable pity party peers. Realistically speaking, your girl talk with your girlfriends doesn't amount to much more than a pity party; a pity party that's rated X. What good can come from that?

~

You don't have to stop your "kit-kat, chit chat" sessions with your buddies. No, by all means continue your girl talk, as men too will continue with locker room talk. Just keep in mind what you have just read. To reiterate, try hard to find a way to include your man in your girl talk. If you succeed in telling him what's said during the meeting in the ladies room, you won't have to spend so much time fantasizing with friends. You'll be fantasizing and realizing with your **MAN**.

~

OUT OF THE BLUE

When I set out to write this book, the first thing I was asked by the few ladies I spoke with beforehand was, "where do I look to find a good black man?" Single women asked me that question as if I could really answer it, and as if that were the crux of my book. Sure, I'd like to be able to pinpoint the exact locations for you to frequent, in order to find your Mr. Right. I'd like to be able to say, "O.K., Terri, go to this church on this particular day and he'll be waiting for you in the lobby." Or, "Alice, attend this concert at this arena and he'll be there." Or, "Toni, hang out at the museum and you'll bump into the man of your dreams." As much as I would like to offer every reader this service, I am realistic enough to know that it just can't be done. I'm not in the crystal ball business.

~

In fact I won't even go so far as to say what

types of places. Rather, the need should be stressed that you must know where you are in this life. Someone once said, "You can't know where you're going unless you know where you are." As you know, the key to map reading is knowing where you are, at the present moment. A point of reference is needed if you are to successfully navigate any given territory. If you're lost in a shopping mall, the very first thing you look for on the customer courtesy map is the "YOU ARE HERE" arrow. "Ah, so here's Sears and there's Foot Locker and here I am. So to get to Penney's I have to take this route." You know how it goes. The same is true of finding a mate, only the map is not on a handy pamphlet or on some board at the end of a hallway. The map is within you, and your job is to look deep within to find out where you are on that map.

~

Where are you? Do you know? One thing is for certain, you will never find a good man, until you first find yourself.

~

I'll invoke the powerful lyrics of the Queen of Hip Hop Soul, Mary J. Blige, from the tune "Be Happy." She cries yearningly, " I wanna be so happy, but the answer lies in me." She also sings, "How can I love somebody else, if I can't love myself enough to know..." It basically boils down to that. Nothing fancy. No hocus pocus, love beads, candles, oil, tarot cards, Ouija boards, psychics, or palm readers. A magic lamp won't help you either. Inner focus is the key. Take a long concentrated look at yourself. It's that simple (easier said than done, I'm sure).

There is something that we must inject into this conversation that is probably more important than anything I've said thus far. I must mention the God component. That's right, the bottom line to your finding a decent man to share your life with rests firmly in the all-pervasive, unseen hand of the Creator of the universe. God. This is not to say that you should abandon all your efforts at preparing yourself for the man of your dreams. No, by all means you must remain diligent in your preparatory program, for it is this preparation that will allow you to recognize and keep Mr. Right. However, the date, the time, the season and the circumstance of your anticipated encounter with your prospective mate will be determined by forces that are way beyond your mortal control. You may call it God, fate or luck. Call it what you will (I'll call this God), but you must know that ultimately your man will appear suddenly, unexpectedly and totally out of the blue.

~

You might run across him while waiting to get your car out of the shop; you may find him while jogging at the health club; he might accidentally graze up against you in a department store; maybe for a change, he decides to take the commuter train you ride everyday and comes and sits right by you. Or perhaps he'll just appear out of thin air.
You never know.

~

The key -- and this is the absolute essence of this book -- is to be ready when he enters your life and to know how to keep him when he's there. Chances are, this has probably been your biggest problem in your search for a man. You have either not been ready when Mr. Right stepped right up to you, or you had him and couldn't keep him. If you're alone right now, that is probably the reason why. I simply refuse to believe that you've never had a chance at a good man. A lot of women tell that lie. "Ain't no good men out there, girl," they say with absolute finality. They're just as wrong as they can be. So don't you buy into that myth, and moreover don't propagate it. The truth is, there are scores of good men out there. There's at least one good one out there looking for you right now. But are you ready for him? Ready...for when he comes from out of the blue?

~ The Beginning ~

APPENDIX

SISTERS AND STATISTICS

In the United States, there are approximately 10 Black women to every 7 Black men.

In the 30-34 year old age group, there are 180,000 more Black women than Black men.

On a college campus, the female-to-male ratio among Blacks is 2 to 1 and among whites it is 6 to 5. Some campuses can have up to 2,4, or even 6 Black women for every 1 Black man.

The city of Buffalo in New York is probably the worst city for single Black women. There are 152 Black women for every 100 Black men.

African-Americans are the only ethnic group in which a majority of children live with single mothers (62% or 5.6 million children).

The Best City for Black Women (Ages 18-34)

City	Men	Women
San Diego, CA	23,374	13,442

Other good cities for sisters are Norfolk, New Orleans, Baltimore, Los Angeles, Houston, Philadelphia, and Oakland.

Sources: USA Today July 1993, Ebony July 1993, Essence March 1995, Statistical Abstract 1991.

Epilogue

There is a writer in everyone, but few put pen to pad. Ted, you did it. This book was once just an idea in the minds of the Positive People staff and look what happened. And to think, most people know you as a great singer...not a writer. I praise God for giving me the wisdom to know the difference between talking a good game and publishing a good book. When He calls you, you better respond. As God is my witness, I pontificate in the words of the Psalms of David, "The Lord Gave the Word: and Great was the company of those that published it." (68:11).

God Bless All of You

Garrard McClendon
Publisher

Thoughts

Thoughts

Thoughts